Phantom Gothic

Iron Fist

By

Spike Bloodworth

First published by AuthorHouse 09/16/04

ISBN: 1-4184-7076-7 (e-book)
ISBN: 1-4184-5356-0 (Paperback)

This book is printed on acid free paper.

HONORABLE MENTIONS

DEREK DAYTON, ERNESTINE OAKS,
KIMBERLI DIX, JAMES REEVES,
ANNE RAMIREZ, BRIAN LIDDLE,
RYAN & CHRISTINA PIERCE,
JOSEPH DONNELLY, BRYAN PAPE,
CHRISTOPHER, CHRIS WHY,
JOANNE BIGELOW, COREY & CLAY CRIST,
DORIAN RICHARDS, KENT GREG,
FRED RONALLO, JASON DAKE,
AND EVERY GOTHIC UNMENTIONED WHO
BELIEVED…
(the list was too long for every name here.)

TITLE GRAPHICS DONE BY:
LUKE JOHNS

PHOTOGRAPHY DONE BY:
NIKKIE MOORE.

<u>CAREFULLY GUARDED</u>

Just leave me alone and get on with your life,
once I am burned don't think we'll be friends twice.
I can forgive but I can never forget,
'cause once I take you back you'll only do it again.
What I do not need is to have myself to defend,
by guilt of your actions by affiliation or association.
The best way to be is carefully guarded,
a lesson hard learned.
I won't be embarrassed by the idiot nation,
won't allow them all to start taking their turns.
I've had enough and I want out now,
'cause lesser beings need to be less stupid but they
don't know how.
You could tell them a hundred different ways;
tell them until you are blue in the face every day,
"I am not to be messed with."
I am carefully guarded.

Spike Bloodworth

<u>CREEP</u>

Got a fascination with things mildly morbid,
amused by the bizarre.
But no matter how much I may seem sick & twisted,
I don't encourage mayhem and murder.
Anarchy is alright by me,
without upheaval and violence.
Call me a pervert or creep,
there's a limit to my vindictiveness.
What I speak for shock value,
that's never motivated by malice.
So accuse me of being disturbed,
simply because I am different.
But at least you don't need a clean up crew from the
morgue or the sanitation department.

MAKING IT GOSPEL

Making it gospel to never owe anyone any favors,
if I do it then I do it through my own free will.
My honor system…
you honor it also.
If I go above and beyond,
that is kindness not overkill.
Exceed my expectations,
the offers I offer do not refuse.
I do it not to be overbearing, self imposing or rude.
If self sacrifice is my law and code,
(so be it) there is no indignity involved.
I learned resourcefulness as a mere child,
struggling through scarcity no more, those days are
gone.
Making it gospel never to deny those in need to the
very best of my ability,
I am trading places.
The scars of depravity are grooved so deep,
that to turn my back on those who ask even the
smallest of things,
is to do that which I hate:
the "you're only using me." routine.
I understand you don't want to be obligated to
returning complicated favors,
so when I offer them I expect nothing in return,
I give you my word.

Spike Bloodworth

<u>SHAPESHIFTER</u>

You ever notice those people who never speak to
anyone unless they absolutely must?
Who don't move around but simply sit back and
WATCH.
No facial expression and no hint of thought,
BEWARE! you have **no idea** what they are capable of!
They are the kind that will ambush you in battle,
they never let their secrets out.
They are the bigger and tougher fish,
and easy to underestimate if you are a fool.
They appear to be the one you are up against,
and suddenly appears an entire army and arsenal.
Those are the ones you approach on their terms and
conditions,
and you never chance getting on their less gallant side.
If this sounds a little farfetched,
it would only take one wrong move – no matter how
small – to change your mind.
I did that only **once** when I was young,
and ambled off with badly mangled pride.

<u>SEVERED</u>

Blessed creature,
innocent yet inflicted,
Be free from pain,
free from torture and sleeplessness evermore,
Be cleansed and pure.
Stay this way for an eternity.
Peace is my gift to you little beast,
no one ever deserved a healing more.

<u>RAISING A REVOLT</u>

I have spoken,
the ruler of my own universe.
The decider of my own destiny,
the one who voices to the overlords what everyone else
is
thinking yet they dare not speak.
The overlords dislike the heaviness of my presence.
I was a born leader,
the one they do not hesitate to follow.
They know who to designate to put the pressure on the
overlords,
I have become a one "man" show.
The people do not have to fear the wrath of the
overlords,
no probability of getting beheaded.
Still, they hesitate to show their positions of
resentment,
to risk the removal of food on the table instead.
It is not a show of weakness to defend your daily
bread.
However,
what edifies the body is only a stepping stone to the
strengthening of the spirit.

SKELETONS IN THE CLOSET

People ask me all the time "What is a Gothic?"
"What constitutes being one?"
my answer will always baffle them,
it is "Skeletons in the closet."
We are survivors of dysfunctional families and
traumatic events.
Events like this:…
A child is locked in a dark closet with cardboard
skeletons
because they have refused to take a nap.
My mother's once alive puppy is lying on the living
room floor with a snapped neck,
a note is scrawled "this could have been you." attached
to the body (my father was that violent).
A younger sister is watching cartoons while our
parents are having a heated argument.
To get even with our mother he picks the girl up by the
hair and throws her into another room.
She cries but there is nothing I can do.
A chunk of her hair was still in the palm of his hands,
need I say more or have you gotten the point yet?

<u>TAKING THE BITTER OFFENSIVE</u>

I cannot prevent you from clinging to your niche
amongst the walking wounded,
since your playthings walked away I can only admit
they were insensitive.
They aren't thinking about you so give up the ghost of
them,
and I will assist you in forgetting it ever happened.
Because the day the last relationship ended was the day
you should've moved on,
and instead of taking the bitter offensive you should
have made room for new love.
Everyone sometime or another feels robbed and
swindled in matters of the heart,
I am no exception to the rule.
But here's the deal and I hope you are listening
intently,
because the day your last relationship ended they
promptly gave up the ghost of you.
So you can drown your sorrows in gin and tonic,
or become a workaholic, to no benefit.
Or there is the obvious alternative,
to stop taking the bitter offensive.

<u>DARTS</u>

If I had a picture for everyone who was unreliable,
who didn't know up from down;
who did what they will and deserted me,
it would cover several entire walls.
I can assure you each and every picture
would be riddled with holes.
I'd toss those torpedoes in when I was bored,
hammer them in when angry as Hell.
Replace the old one with new faces once in a while,
or burn them to a crisp and watch them fall to the
ground.
Would line those likenesses up from ceiling to floor;
even though I despise each and every one,
cringe to even look at them,
I'd demolish them to unrecognizability anyhow.
After all I do need to get the disappointment out of my
system,
need a sense of closure.
How can you cut the ties that bind,
when they walk off flinging you the finger?
If there's one thing I would aspire to most,
it would be that mangled and tattered work of art.

<u>TANTRUMS</u>

She stabs the paper over and over,
stabbed it to oblivion like she just doesn't care.
'Cause the frustration of the day got her feeling pretty
wicked,
and there is no other way to demonstrate how sick of it
she is.
She spews out complaints under every exasperated
breath,
her jaws sore because her teeth are tightly clenched.
This girl is on the brink of wreaking havoc,
and if she didn't have a future who knows what she
would have done.
People tell her all the time to calm down,
to stop looking so angry.
They don't know the **meaning** of the word **ANGRY!**
'cause they have never seen her lose her composure
until now.
This is as explosive as it gets,
so give her plenty of paper until there is none left to
give.
I promise you I have seen this behavior before,
which dies out and goes nowhere.
So all you onlookers just get back to your business,
this little tantrum never took place;
have no fear.

WARNING: CAN CAUSE MILD IRRITATION

There was an advertisement overhead,
it read: "Never shake a baby, ask me why."
The child in the picture was clearly handicapped,
it was meant to make an impact on the passersby.
It certainly did it's job on me,
served it's purpose quite effectively.
But the nearby crowd was not using discretion,
laughing and making disturbing comments.
Someone said: "You can't cause injuries like that
unless you held the child by the feet
and shook it like a carpet."
Another said: "Stirred – not shaken please."
For me the mere mention of child abuse in any form
causes mild irritation.
It **should** be brought to public view,
so the **problem** can be **eliminated.**
but say nothing at all if you're not helping to find a
solution,
because I've been a victim and people who leer and
jest spark up my hatred.

Spike Bloodworth

<u>THE WATCHER</u>

The watcher is your enemy,
scrutinizing every move you make under lock and key.
The watcher is your predator and you have fallen prey,
the day you married him you signed your life away.
"You must call me master when I call you…
my slave…for now you are my property
the day you said the words:
SERVE and **OBEY**."
"Unless you want to make me angry do not question
my authority,
and never question what I do, unless you deny your
own needs,
my personal business does not concern you."

<u>PREDATOR</u>

He takes all you have and leaves you with nothing,
says he loves you but he doesn't know what love
means.
He's controlling you and you give in to his wants,
because he threatens to beat you when you are not.
Why do you call him your better half?
when what you have is not nearly half a man.
For all the injustices he's done,
your physical bruises may heal,
but your mental scars are never gone.
So disappear quietly if you value your pathetic life,
if you stay there any longer you are surely going to die.

<u>IT</u>

I announced "I'm pregnant, now what do you want me
to do about this?"
That day he'd rather see me dead.
"Abort – get rid of it."
Not him…not her…or the child,
that would be murder.
Not the boy…not the girl…not the baby,
then **it** could feel.
No, **it** came from me so **it** doesn't deserve to live.
So I took my stand and packed my bags,
(fuck him) his drinking, drugs and other women.
This child is mine and mine alone from this day
forward,
her smile will shine because there is life in her.
He is nothing and no one,
has nothing and no one,
and without him we did fine for 6 years.

<u>READ THE SPINAL COLUMN</u>

The girl had a twisted spine at a very young age,
her foster parents took no notice of her potential pain.
She knew they weren't loaded but she's still a ward of
the state,
so how do these things slip by in such inappropriate
ways?
Well now she's got pinched nerves now that she's a
grown woman,
and speaking up for herself gained her nothing before
it happened.
Can't say I'm impressed with the way parents show
love to their children by ignoring them.
It's a long way to go to change this kind of situation,
'cause **survival of the fittest** should not be the first
lesson taught to children.
There are millions out there abandoned and lonesome,
trying to escape to public paradises to avoid the
nonexistent warmth of home.
Parents are gods to an infant when their first milestone
words are spoken.
Getting conceived was not their decision.
Let this not be forgotten.

Spike Bloodworth

CLASH OF THUNDER

There we stood in the corner,
day after day / hour after hour.
This is our punishment,
it keeps us weak and tired.
You can see her fury,
as we cringe from her tyrant brutality.
We duck the blows automatically,
like the cat whose tail is stepped on one time too many.
In her murderous rage she pulled our hair,
ignoring our whimpers of pain,
her loss of control escalated,
then the clash of heads and thunder came.
Our bodies took a daily bruising and beating,
our gruesome reality.
Now that she is gone I have no love or grief for her –
our dearly departed mother.

<u>CALAMITY JANE</u>

I'm pleased to meet you,
just call me Calamity.
That's the best word that describes me, although I've
always disliked the fact immensely.
I find it quite unjust,
because I've never done anything to deserve it.
The day I was born misfortune decided to latch onto
me,
that's a shame you know because I have so much
potential it really is a pity.
Farewell you say? are you going to leave already?
Yes, well I predicted you wouldn't stay.
People rarely do when they hear what I have to say.
May God guide you, bless you and lead you to safety.

<u>WICKED SELECTIVE</u>

You have selective hearing child and there is animosity
between us,
but you forget that I too was a child once.
I had things all figured out before I was graced with
your presence,
so there is just no way I will continue to bend over
backwards.
Go ahead and learn your lessons the hard way,
I will keep my distance.
And when you are done making a spectacle of
yourself,
then come back and we will speak the same language.
In the future I will choose my battles more wisely and
with a wicked vengeance.

GRIMACE

I came to you when I fell apart,
you patted me on the shoulder as a sympathetic
gesture;
because you knew what was in my heart.
You will never know how something so small can be
like a sunlit winter thaw.
I grimaced under that speaker at the words to your
favorite song.
So I think of you whenever you fall apart,
and how Kiss the Rain is such a beautiful song,
because at that moment it was on and made me realize
how wonderful you were all along.

Spike Bloodworth

<u>QUOTED VERBATUM</u>

I know that warning tone,
it's the compliment before the fall.
That warning tone alone tells me all there is to know.
There is something weighing heavily on your mind
you would rather not say at all.
You plan to let me off easy;
don't waste your time on the cowardly way to appease
me.
Yes – I can imitate that callous monotone,
I'll even quote you verbatum.
Either choice I make I lose with the choices I've been
given.
So now that you have my undivided attention,
you don't have to kick me like a dog to make me run
any faster.
But do expect the one you do kick to avoid your eyes
and whimper.
I hope someday you suffer through the very same
ultimatum,
the exact one we are both quoting verbatum.

AMBUSHED

She doesn't see it coming the poor little unsuspecting
creature,
how can she bear to live with me as I am cracking
under pressure?
Sometimes I can't control it (the more I fight it) the
harder and faster it comes.
Sometimes no matter how much I warn her;
use my words and try to tone down my anger,
she just ignores my warnings.
It's like that child does not care,
she just wants to do things her way.
I feel ambushed and defensive.
I can't avoid feeling bitter,
like a complete and utter failure.

Spike Bloodworth

<u>DUALITY</u>

You don't know me intimately,
or should I say as much as you'd like to believe?
Lately I haven't divulged any intricate details and
we're opposites on everything.
I prefer not to reveal things that can be used against
me,
because instead of living like a charmed individual,
I must breathe a life of duality.
It puts a strain on our friendship but it serves me more
wisely.

<u>ROLLING THE CLOSING CREDITS</u>

I don't give you enough credit for your moral support,
when you lift me above all obstacles to overcome fear.
I may forget to thank you or show appreciation,
but I do notice when you drop everything to listen with a
sympathetic ear.
So please forgive me for acting like a selfish jerk,
I regret treating you like dirt and not allowing you to
shine through.
Because I am nothing, absolutely nothing, without you.

Spike Bloodworth

I'M NOT OUT TO IMPRESS YOU

I'm not out to impress you,
not putting my life on the line,
I worked so hard just to get here and without you I'm
doing fine.
Just go away and leave me alone (you aren't my type.)
Sooner or later you will get the message,
and you can call it whatever you like.
I started something I can't finish,
that's just the way it is,
I was never out to impress you and wish I never did.

<u>DEPRIVED</u>

It's been proven people die from lack of love,
robbed of all emotions such as gentle words or touch.
It's like searching for acceptance like an abandoned child
looking at stone cold faces that never smile.
Those who avoid looking at you always have and never will,
as if to do so would make you feel worthwhile.
You do not know what you need to survive,
you have no more will to live because you've been deprived.

<u>MOTHER'S DAY</u>

I quit,
I'm outta here;
I can't take it anymore!
This is the only holiday I can't keep my composure.
I'm going to jail myself in my bedroom chamber next
year.
I will order take out food for all three meals,
so I will have no need whatsoever to go outside.
If I hear "Happy Mother's Day!" once more I'll burst
into tears,
I can't watch another child and their parents walk by.
My God! I sometimes wonder how a woman who
wanted children but miscarried feels.
Am I the only woman willingly casting herself into
seclusion?
There's nothing more wretched than giving birth to a
child no longer residing at home,
when you'd give just about anything to give them one
more hug.
My daughter knows I'm alive, but I sacrificed my title
as mom.
Now she calls someone else mother (her only natural
response)
thus I do not receive the customary card.

<u>TARANTULAS</u>

I must resist the temptation to put tarantulas in your
bed,
because I've pictured it a thousand times in my head.
These traumatizing events leave too lasting an
impression,
and alas I must escape eternal damnation.
The things I list, all of them you deserve in this
lifetime not the next:
How about tarantulas crawling on your flesh?
I'd like to see your terror beneath the surface.
You deserve the intimidation of an insect,
a lasting look at death.
You deserve to be destroyed and yet you continue to
live,
I leave it in God's hands.

<u>BESIEGED</u>

Cornered by a thousand different responsibilities,
and the world is a blur from whirlwind activity.
Just know that I am fine no matter what duration I
remain unseen.
You can call on me any time
(I'm here for you heart and soul)
and always will be.
No matter what I am occupied with at the time
(I'll drop it on the dime)
in the interest of compassion and sympathy.
No news is good news,
no time is a good time.
It is amazing that I find time to sleep.
Although I am besieged incessantly,
and although I can rarely be reached,
it will all come to a screeching halt when you call on
me.

<u>NOT EXACTLY</u>

Wait and hear what I have to say before you come to a
conclusion,
it may not be what you expect.
I can see you have already made some assumptions,
which are not exactly what I was going to say next.
So just stay quiet and pay closer attention,
that is the way you show proper respect.

<u>BANISHED</u>

Vanished, without a trace.
Intruders came and invaded my space.
A recluse,
no intentions to go outside,
within my own household I know I must hide.
A missing person,
(don't bother to report)
won't answer the telephone,
won't answer the door.
Those who cannot accept the word no,
they are not welcome anywhere near my home.
I will summon you when I'm ready,
when banishing myself is no longer a need.

<u>PHASE OUT</u>

A crumbled friendship and kinship gone awry,
I'll call you later maybe when I've got the time.
I've always had the time but that doesn't change the
hurt I feel inside,
and maybe someday when I've cooled off I will really
try.
I simply view you as a challenge,
too much resistance in my tides.
Your timing is unfortunate,
it pulls me down each time.
Please allow me my personal space,
let me rearrange my life.
Let me have some peace now so success for once is
mine.
Then I won't phase you out and you won't worry me
blind.

<u>OVERSIMPLIFIED</u>

Please don't ask me to expose the awful, honest truth,
it's too harsh and abrasive to reveal right this moment
to you.
If I spell out bluntly your wakeup call it will slap you
in the face,
Denial is the only notion you will want to embrace,
God as my witness I am glad I am not in your place,
if I were in your shoes I would feel the same.
But I guess I cannot betray my loyalty to you,
and although it pains me to say it,
here is the truth and nothing but the truth…

THE STING

He used to be so vibrant,
so adventurously exciting,
He was never hesitant and always glad to see me.
He used to be so positive,
projecting a fresh point of view.
Around him I really **lived,**
everything was fresh and new.
I wrote him a letter,
told him how fascinating he is,
that love lurked in the air,
especially toward him.
He shirked it and shoved it aside,
brushed me off,
and before I knew what happened I was feeling lost.
Now he avoids me and I feel the **sting.**
If I knew it would end up like this I never would have
written the damned thing!

Spike Bloodworth

<u>YOUR SELF-DEFEATING ATTITUDE</u>

You can't bring me down with your doubt and your
has beens,
reminding me the past only repeats itself.
If that truly is the only advice you can give,
you are no help at all.
That only shows me you expect me to accept defeat,
and I will not drop what I am doing so easily.
I'm no quitter and on that you can depend,
a poet so divine, so excellent.
It may sound far off in the future or impossible,
I can wait and see until I'm dead.
Your self-defeating attitude will humble you,
I am not so negative.
So thankful I'm not like you or blindsighted enough to
respect what you said.

<u>HIGHER STANDARDS</u>

When I chose you as my other half,
I thought this time I had higher standards.
For once I could be thankful for who I am,
since you were not the usual bastard.
But you can't seem to make up your mind if you are
out or in,
are you coming or going?
Because to me we make a perfect fit,
and I thought this time I found someone worthy of
affection,
someone I could give my fullest attention.
You managed to crush all of my hopes,
exiting almost as quickly as you entered in.
In this manner you have proven yourself defective
after all in the end.

Spike Bloodworth

<u>SHE'S YANKIN' YOUR CHAIN</u>

One minute she wants you and doesn't the next,
she likes to play with your emotions to mess with your
head.
She's yankin' your chain and yankin' it hard,
jerkin' you around (your just rewards!)
You come when she calls like a faithful dog,
then she drives you away when she wants you gone.
As your best friend I've seen it all,
I'm the girl you turn to when she forces you to fall.
I am so disappointed 'cause you know you can do
better,
she'll continue to hurt you,
but only if you <u>let</u> her.
She'll tighten her grip on your reigns until the day you
realize she's yankin' your chain.

I'M ELATED

It's been a knockout drag down kind of day,
and I've been begging for it to end.
It didn't start out this way,
with me horrified and disgusted.
So you come along at just the most inconvenient
moment wanting to share your success.
You want to tell me all about it,
since these moments are so rare you can hardly contain
your excitement.
I answer "It's about time! I'm happy for you, elated!"
Your face falls to the floor so discouraged and
crestfallen,
thinking I'm jealous or disinterested.
I responded without much effort or hesitation.
So perhaps with more enthusiasm I should have simply
said "congratulations!"

Spike Bloodworth

<u>GRIPPING</u>

Partners,
Lovers,
two people bonded together.
Sometimes they say things they do not mean,
they both aim it at each other.
So I try to drown out my sorrows and plug music in
my ears.
Often times they are too unforgiving,
relentlessly bitter.
When they first met it was not an all out war,
love back then was flawless.
I can't bear to see them tear each other's heart out
anymore.
Won't they see that "I'm sorry." can seal it all with a
kiss?

<u>FAULTLINES</u>

"It's all my fault, it's all my fault."
"Nothing I do is ever right!"
That's the way the course of our conversation went last
night.
I've never seen so much self pity,
never heard such remorse in all my life.
The things he did were not even remotely
unpardonable,
but just to mention it chokes him up inside.
How many people did all they could to break this man?
to rip away every ounce of pride he had.
How many did that to him and don't deserve to live?
Who raised their voices or fists too often?
Indefinitely he'll be a basket case with an inadequacy
complex!
When do these people recognize they reduced this man
to shreds?
When does their callousness go away and this man gets
some respect?
When do his faultlines run less deep?
So the man reports he got all the sleep he needs.
And last – but certainly not least – when can I hold
him in my arms to stroke his hair and keep him warm,
with a soft genuine smile on his face brought there by a
feeling of peace?!

Spike Bloodworth

BACKBONE

Have a little backbone and clean up your own mess,
start coming to your own defense.
Apologize and repent,
confess your own sins.
Have a little backbone and show the full extent of your
courage,
settling for nothing but the best.
Have some backbone,
get it all in the open right now,
and get it all off your chest.
Hold yourself in the highest regards,
take on your role of leadership.
Don't hesitate one minute more,
make a full impact.
Make your own demands, slam your fist on the desk!

<u>ISSUES</u>

She fired up with "Don't interfere, I've got issues.
I can work them out on my own,
I'm not hiding from the truth."
I've got news for her,
everyone needs a little privacy;
but she is hiding from the truth that hers are not <u>private</u>
issues.
I do have some say in <u>this:</u>
ignorance (of all things) is **not** bliss!
She recants with "I do not need your approval or
permission."
Just denial sanctioned beneath defensiveness.
Her rehabilitation needs a substitute backup plan,
should also include a friend.
Making excuses will only keep the quality of her life
inadequate,
and with her back to a corner with my finger pointed at
her chest she'll never piece together
details that don't fit.
She needs to reprioritize her values,
allowing her newfound knowledge to settle in.

Spike Bloodworth

<u>GUILTLESS</u>

Whatever task I've performed in the past was done
fully aware of the consequences,
I have no regrets for actions done in the past or the
present.
I continue forward without a blemished conscience,
for I have not brought another human to harm.
I stand firmly glued to my convictions,
ingrained entirely by a pure heart.
Nowhere is it permitted for anyone to challenge this,
that door is nailed permanently shut.
Wickedness lacks allure,
especially amongst the many other tempted.
I prefer to stay guiltless.
Because at least I know exactly where I stand.

<u>FRICTION</u>

You are causing me friction,
way too much friction,
I want you out of my life.
Get out of my vision,
far out of my vision,
Don't come back until I say it's time.
How you can provoke so much disgust out of one
person is beyond my comprehension;
it doesn't take much to get me spiraling in deep
depression.
That is something I desire to avoid at all costs,
since I want to feel like the lucky one who still came
out on top.
I've done all the maturing necessary,
now it's time for you to grow up.

Spike Bloodworth

<u>KEEP IT REAL</u>

He sees something that cannot be fixed,
a flaw that never truly existed within my own
personality.
He is mistaken,
attempting to cast his own shadow over me.
He and I are not one and the same,
I do not reflect hypersensitivity and increased
abundances of feelings of futility.
My laid back attitude takes work,
and separation from anxiety.
Seriousness does not get the better of me.
I am not maladjusted like he is,
simply misunderstood by the mainstream.
He, on the other hand, is something broken that can
never be fixed,
thus I suspect that is all he will ever be.

<u>**PRIVELEDGED**</u>

Friends and family make you do things you'll later
regret,
then act like you owe them and you owe them big.
In disbelief I hear this,
in disbelief I shake my head.
I decided long ago to rule my own actions,
because living by someone else's standards won't
satisfy me in the end.
Dangling unconditional love on a string like a carrot;
that's all it comes to,
a lifelong power trip.
No thanks people, I'm too priveledged.

Spike Bloodworth

<u>REMIND ME NEVER TO…</u>

Speak to you again or call you a friend,
say hello or goodbye or come to your defense.
Remind me never to…
dwindle on the good times or rehash on all the bad,
or forsake the things that are mine for things I never
truly had.
Just don't come around here at all,
don't bother to pick up the phone and call.
All I want is solitude within my four walls,
and I will do whatever it takes to preserve my peace.
So I can do without you now and forever to make my
unease cease.

__SINKING FAST__

Your thoughts are heavy,
I can sense it from across the room.
I know when you came in,
know when you are gone.
I am everywhere,
I am inside your head.
You can release yourself and relax,
you're better off not thinking at all if all it brings you
is unhappiness.
I enter the picture when the clouds obstruct the ceiling,
wherever the air is thick.
You look as if you've seen a ghost,
as if I've pushed you back.
Don't you know how intense your thought pattern
really is?
It screams help me I'm sinking fast!
It leaks out and hisses in fact,
A person would have to be wrapped up in themself not
to respond to that.

Spike Bloodworth

<u>WHATEVER</u>

You tell me what I don't want to hear,
it will all sink in later.
Don't force the issue,
I will only back up in reverse.
You tell me what I don't want to hear,
I'll shrug my shoulders and say "Whatever!!!"
It's all just a lot of inflated hot air,
in one ear and out the other.
You sweat the small stuff all the time,
I sweat it no further.
Things are too maximized by your standards,
it's none of my concern.
Take it easy, don't cause yourself an ulcer.

<u>SEARCH AND SEIZURE</u>

When Sticky Fingers strikes he takes all I own away,
takes it all and leaves me with nothing.
Sometimes he takes it all in one day,
that's damn frustrating!!!
I see no reason why I slave away my life,
while Sticky Fingers snatches away my possessions in
the middle of the night.
It makes me wonder if I am safe at home alone and just
who I can protect.
Since Sticky Fingers lurks in the shadows with things I
had no chance to enjoy yet!

Spike Bloodworth

FRIENDS AS ENEMIES/ENEMIES FOR FRIENDS

Don't need a list of my shortcomings they are already
evident,
no one knows each one better than I do,
I am the cause of them.
You don't need to point out my faults,
I know I am imperfect.
If I did the same to you,
how you would resent the fact!
I can tell you how you would react,
recoiling in horror would be the only after effect.
So don't ruin my high regard of you,
while I thought you had more class.
Don't forsake our closeness for absence,
while my faultlines may be obvious,
it's also obvious that enemies don't make good friends.

<u>SARCASM</u>

I just don't understand where your confusion lays,
how can you miss whether I am serious or not?
My sarcasm is straight to the point,
and my point always gets across.
I've never spoken in riddles and roundabout ways,
there's no possibility of getting lost.
I say what I mean, even in comedy,
no holds barred.
No need to search for deeper meanings,
the slapstick is slapping you in the face.
No need for repetition,
you heard me correctly in the first place.
You can see for yourself how painfully direct my
statements are made,
I'll never be the one to withhold the truth and let you
learn the hard way.
The timing is never awkward,
I avoid altogether off color flippant styles.
Condescending tones aren't necessary,
just look for a sardonic smile.
you can see for yourself how painfully direct my
statements are made.
I'll never be the one to withhold the truth,
to let you be the one who learned things the hard way.

<u>SANCTUARY</u>

There's no room to breathe and no truce for peace,
you're never alone anymore.
There's no time to sleep and no time to just "be",
there's nothing left of you anymore.
It's the same old daily routine with no place to retreat,
(like somewhere behind closed doors).
Although you're dead beat and still on your feet
despite your ghostly pallor,
you watch yourself age twenty years as you inspect
your face in the mirror.
Where is your permanent sanctuary?
you ask yourself, baptizing your face in cold water.
Where is your place to flee civilization and people who
devour your power?
All you need is privacy, open country and time to
smell the flowers.

<u>EMBLAZONED IN BOLD PRINT</u>

It's not that everything I say is not important,
it most certainly is.
There's a few things that must be reinforced however,
and those are the things emblazoned in bold print.
I don't feel things must flash out at you in neon lights,
but some people take extra effort to get the message.
There are many I have met who do not take in much of
their surroundings,
oblivious to even the most crucial details.
They are the ones who do not travel far outside their
homes,
perhaps they are also the ones afraid of microbes.
They shrug their shoulders and instantaneously answer
"Whatever."
to just about every question directed to them.
I seriously doubt there is much they can benefit from,
I don't have much to offer.
If they picked up this book, scanned the title and never
read so much as a solitary chapter,
then that's their loss and my gain;
let them suffer.

Spike Bloodworth

<u>DECOMPOSED</u>

She cries in public,
no one else has the balls to do that!
Her misery is making her crack,
I admire her courage too,
because everyone else is confusing it for drama and
turning their backs.
She knows shedding those tears is senseless,
exacting revenge is useless and going forward must
come from within.
Any other day she is so strong,
unless some fool is jerking her around.
It's too tempting to sell your soul,
to stay young and well preserved,
to never grow old,
but she won't sell out to a vanishing promise, thus
sometimes she deserves to be decomposed.

ONE MORE CHANCE

I don't know what happened here but I almost had one
less friend,
and I'm not sure exactly what went wrong but I do
know I don't want that.
I'm willing to apologize although I suspect I'm not the
one who is wrong,
I'm sure we can work it out and turn this situation back
around.
I miss the good times and all the fun we had,
so here I am begging you to give me one more chance.
You see there is one thing I realize even now,
that I won't get anywhere thinking in terms of holier
than thou.
Begging takes bravery and humbleness to submit,
and mockery may be my reward, I will take that
chance.

Spike Bloodworth

<u>TIME LAPSE</u>

Took the day off from work in memory of you,
with you above all in my mind and heart.
I did it to honor you on your birthday,
although we are many miles apart.
We may be separated for many years,
you won't observe my actions.
But I do them to heal in a healthy way for your benefit,
and maybe someday I may discontinue this unobserved
tradition.
Only on the day discomfort and disconcerted feelings
stop bubbling to the surface.
I love you….you are not soon forgotten.

<u>STICKLER</u>

Sure…use that condescending tone as if I am an idiot,
walk me through your thought process as if we don't
speak the same language.
Speak nice and slow and paternize me with every
sentence,
and look at me like you just spoke to a person with
minimal intelligence.
And when you are done with your condescending
ways,
look into my face and see my well contained rage.
I will reply that "I got to the point far **AHEAD** of you
<u>before</u> you explained it."
"Therefore, I do not **have** to **like** it
and **<u>still</u>** showing you **undeserved** respect."
Once I've put you back in your place you will shrink
back looking and feeling like you just
got slapped.

<u>BILE</u>

I hate you and if you died tomorrow I doubt I would
give a damn,
it doesn't really matter anyway 'cause I'm as bitter as I
sound like I am.
All I know is hostility, bloodlust and rage,
too bad it is all restricted to words across this page.
This isn't aimed at you the reader but more like my
enemies,
if I could line them all up and shoot them I could do so
quite well with ease.
It may be against the law,
at least I am not above that.
I dwell in the realm of reality,
but just between you and me I would rather not be.
Some people deserve horrors worse than death,
what they give is not what they get back.
I believe in the death penalty,
for murderers, rapists and such.
They did not deserve to live in the first place,
and their next victim in line cannot leave it for God to
judge.

PREMATURE GOODBYES

Maybe I forwarded you too much respect,
so I resort to reminding myself I never truly knew
you in the end.
Influenced myself into thinking you were a potential
candidate for a friend,
when I should've known from the start it would cause
me regret.
I put you on a pedestal where you'd rather not be,
something that should be treated as an honor when
done by me.
Your loss is my gain with your premature goodbyes on
your breath,
it made me realize your company serves no purpose.

<u>INADEQUATE</u>

If it were not you it would've been someone else,
a story so predictable I know it far too well.
We enter and exit this world with NOTHING,
which is something far above your understanding.
You doubt a person can be impoverished and still have
any worth,
yet you will enter and exit the very **same way** from
this Earth.
It is not pleasurable and not of my choosing,
so I cannot defend a past that was none of my doing.
Easier it is to stay judgemental.
I may be inadequate by **human** standards,
but many life sustaining things come from the dirt.
It is not my origins that are hurtful,
since you were protected and provided for from the
day of your birth.

<u>WARPATH</u>

You're shaking me hard like a soda bottle,
my anger goes up and comes down violent and at full
throttle.
I'm feeling mighty powerful and forceful,
I don't need a witness or audience when I explode.
So cover your ears and eyes 'cause I'm on the warpath
now.
I'm telling you now I think you better go,
go this very second,
GET OUT! GET OUT! GET OUT!

Spike Bloodworth

<u>PRAISEWORTHY</u>

Smiles everyone smiles!
Places everyone now take your places!
We must absolutely disguise ourselves as happy.
We have appearances to keep in public you know,
no matter how painful or unhealthy.
I congratulate you all for being here,
putting in your best efforts,
for dragging your lifeless bodies through this routine,
proving yourselves praiseworthy.
Visibly you sometimes tire of pretending to be lively,
you deserve a pat on the back nonetheless,
incredible how dedicated you've all been lately!

<u>REMAIN INCONSPICUOUS</u>

Don't tell anyone anything,
just remain inconspicuous.
The less you reveal the less they know,
your friendships will stay continuous.
Nevermind that this behaviour is incoherent,
(not to mention utterly ridiculous)
I was taught if you are a wallflower you will go
unnoticed,
but these days it seems exactly the opposite.
Nevermind that you are penalized for things beyond
your control,
if you were ever a victim just don't tell others so.
If you ever experienced dread or weakness,
you are perceived as a damaged soul,
and if you ever voice it,
you will forever stay alone.

Spike Bloodworth

BOILING BLOOD

The heat is rising to my face,
both fists clenched tight at my sides.
I am absolutely livid,
you can see the boiling blood rise.
Usually so calm/cool/collected,
telling everyone else what to do with the small stuff:
don't sweat it.
She just knows every way to push me past my limits,
it must be written on my forehead!
Maybe she's just evil,
Maybe? Hell – she was born with it!
So now my life force simmers hot and heavy,
I'm thrusting the door open, shoving her out of the
way.
If I could lift her up and pin her to the wall,
oh yeah – that would startle her enough to shut her up
quick,
since I am thinner and stronger (her downfall).
The force I used to burst through the door knocked her
off balance.
I don't think she expected me to have the balls to
intrude as fiercely as I did.
But you know something?
She's a mere girl and I am a woman.
Threatening her with the same insolence would give
me little satisfaction.
So tonight she merely got a scare tactic and the door is still
attached to the hinges.

<u>JAGGED</u>

Been taking the heat from everyone else's grudges,
minor tiffs and jagged edges.
Been jilted from behind enemy lines too many times,
they need to stop interrupting my conversations.
Don't you people have a life to live?!
been answering too many unnecessary questions,
well beyond aggravated.
Ignoring you doesn't make you go away,
even my hair dye is far less permanent.
Daily brain cramps from a battery of assault,
playing the nice guy just to keep up appearances;
when I'd rather tell them all just to f—k off!
Lately I've been wicked jagged,
because I'm tired of the phone ringing off the hook.
A million times a day I want to rip it out of the wall for
good.
Just this once I want to back right out,
because I have better things to do with my life,
better things to do than cater to your needs on every
whim and fancy.
I'd like nothing better right now,
than to tell you my needs are not being met, so maybe
you need to wait also.

<u>SHORTNESS OF BREATH</u>

Aren't you experiencing a shortness of breath?
Aren't you done arguing and complaining yet?
I'm so exasperated with your selfish intent,
milking me for all you can get.
You're how old and you still can't cope?
Just get me a gun and I'll end it for both.
Your misery just makes me flee,
I care enough for 2 not 3.
So do yourself a favor and go favor someone else,
because the verbal offenses you commit widen the
breech.
So don't sour the grapes for all of your foes,
or out the door one by one they will go.

I TOLD YOU SO

You ask me for my advice and then go and do otherwise,
when I've seen and done it all and know your future demise.
I shake my head in the aftermath and wonder what went wrong,
why is so much foolishness so attractive to a person so young?
I'm in the "seen that – done that" phase of life,
seen it all before with my very own eyes.
You cannot say I did not forewarn you because I most certainly did,
and you never heard a word I said!
In one ear and out the other so fast it made your head spin,
and I can just bet you would still go back and make the same mistakes again.
Well before you do I am going to make sure to get the last word in,
'cause when you go out lookin' for trouble you are sure to find it.
And hey – just one more thing before you go…I told you so!!!

Spike Bloodworth

<u>NOBODY'S FREE LUNCH</u>

A homeless man orders breakfast in the local Burger
King,
an everyday occurrence (if you know just what I
mean).
He is silent and keeps to himself,
good food is hard to find.
This introverted person was seeking shelter from the
cold,
with only the meal in front of him on his mind.
While he was minding his own business a policeman
rudely interrupted him,
and refused to allow the man to finish.
The food went to waste,
thrown thoughtless in a trash bin.
Arrested for trespassing he was dumped off in the
middle of nowhere,
a remote place with no warmth or shelter.
Well this lawman never thought he would get caught,
he'll have to pay eventually for what he did wrong.
The homeless man knew his rights,
and it is positively ironic,
that the offender is this case was forced into early
retirement!

<u>MERCY/MERCY</u>

I couldn't stand by your side every hour,
every minute of every day.
I can't promise you comfort or a rich and powerful life,
I can't prevent your suicide attempts,
cut short your demise.
So I guess I am just as compassionless as all the rest,
because my need to survive is an equal conflict of
interest.
You are still turbulent,
I must sustain my engagements.
But my heart is with you always,
even when we are separate.
My only fear is that your attempts will someday be
successful,
and I must live on in guilt.
I tried to coax you out of it,
but you were reluctant to listen.
Everyday you are still alive I am amazed,
miracles really do happen.

<u>IT STOPS HERE</u>

Don't expect pity when you push me away,
as if in your most desparate hour I wasn't there in the
first place.
Don't create your own denial,
shut me out and claim I do not care.
The heartache you feel,
you are the one keeping it there.
I was tender to you once;
once and once only because I got too close.
There was a night I heard you recount the reasons for
your bitterness and hate.
I listened with remorse, knowing I could relate.
But **Alone** would rather stay **Alone**, instead of getting
hurt and risking more pain.
I will be open with you,
now you do the same.
It stops here,
or **self pity** is your **eternal** flame.

SHORT/SWEET

Time is of the essence so make it short and forget the
sweet,
since I'm hearing the same old arguments previously
brought before me.
I find your persistent provocation rather infuriating,
so let this be your final warning.
In retaliation to your efforts (should they continue)
I'll arrest you for trespassing.
This concludes our meeting now,
find your own way out the door for the time being.

Spike Bloodworth

<u>LEECH</u>

There is nothing left of this friendship,
and no matter how I try to keep you at a distance you
repeatedly refuse to accept it.
Someone like me only comes once in a lifetime,
nevertheless you didn't take long to blow it!
Your octopus tentacles never grasp onto my
elusiveness,
never cringe at my crisp vocal sharpness.
Your totally lifeless substance drains away all my
energy,
like a bloodless leech,
as you are sucking dry any feeling I have left!!!

SOMETHING LOST IN THE TRANSLATION

You say one thing yet do another and actions do speak
louder than words.
Maybe you had better choreograph your expressions if
you want to be better heard.
You've got some pretty well hidden agendas since you
don't speak your mind.
That won't just happen between you and me it will
happen all the time.
Unaware of the mixed signals you project,
sending others away in bewildered conflict.
Maybe you should be a little more detailed or specific,
you definitely need to be more direct.
If there's something lost in the translation others do not
know how to react.
Now…Mr. Avoid Conflict at All Costs…What do you
think about that?!

<u>NOTHING HUMOROUS ABOUT HELL</u>

I could sell that sour apple bitterness in a bottle,
you seem to exude it so well.
Carry your body with a rigid stiffness,
telling everyone to go to Hell.
You may shower but you still stink,
the evil inside you even animals can smell.
Better change your ways before the church bells toll,
before the angel of death comes to snatch up your soul.
Death may come sooner than you expect.
it could happen tomorrow.
I sure would hate to see you end up where you tell
everyone else to go,
there's nothing humorous about Hell.

<u>DELINQUENT</u>

Promises / promises from all of you,
nevertheless I won't hold my breath.
'Cause I know you all too well,
and **you are all delinquent.**
Just a bunch of untrustworthy no shows,
and your invisibility is most obvious.
Responsibility for you is a bygone,
you'd rather lose a few friends.
I often wonder how uncalculated you are with your
source of income,
how unreliable are you to your job?
I'm absolutely amazed you got one,
then managed somehow to hang on.
Oh but wait…there's more…lot's more!
Word gets around when you're undependable,
once the verdict is in the label sticks.
All people around you notice is your most prevalent
flaw,
they don't recognize your finer attributes at all.
This is not a double edged sword,
your listeners need to be able to trust you at your word.
Please try to remember that their time is as important
as yours,
it has a great deal of value,
even if it means little or nothing to you.

Spike Bloodworth

<u>UNSPOKEN</u>

Don't be fooled,
you are never alone,
Your cranium is a crowded room.
Beware what you say and how you say it,
during those conversations to yourself,
conversations to yourself contained inside your skull.
Even if it's not vocalized at this very moment,
everyone around you still heard it.
That is how your opponent stays one step ahead,
how the evil ones know what your weakness is;
your thoughts are hanging in the balance unprotected.
Because there is power in every thought and action,
that's why you are uncomfortable when people look at
you so intensely,
almost as if their eyes could pierce your skin.
Nothing is said in secret,
nothing stays well hidden.
Be sure of this, stay cautious.

MANIACAL LAUGHTER

Some say I'm crazy or outright insane,
(downright lost my marbles or not playing with a full
deck again.)
Whichever way you view me it's my plan to falter,
in times of crisis my sides are split with laughter.
Perhaps comedy is not always the correct answer,
but humor is always preferable over disaster.
In medieval times a fool was called a jester or joker,
but in present day laughter is a maniacal gesture.
I insist that in times of grief it is a sigh of relief and
nothing more.

Spike Bloodworth

<u>STABILIZER</u>

I had to leave the horror flick,
that director should get fired.
It's not that I was remotely physically sick,
but who knows what evil that inspires?!
I don't take pleasure in dismemberment, torment or
pain.
Those things are unnatural,
and trapped humans are like animals;
they flinch and they scream.
Being a witness to it makes me just as guilty,
even if only viewing it on a screen.
Vile things make me squirm,
gripping my arm rest I sink low in my seat.
I'm disgusted by the rise in violence,
and the senseless need to see someone bleed.

THE BUTTONHOLE EXPERIMENT

That child is the ultimate tester of patience!
How much further will she go for attention?
What shenanigans will she come up with next?
I am the worst when it comes to emergency situations,
so accordingly I was uptight about the buttonhole
experiment.
Did she do it on purpose or out of sheer ignorance?
I should be fully alert and instead I feel unconscious.
I can accept the fact that children in general are
naturally curious,
but does she absolutely have to shove a button up her
nasal passage?!

<u>**REPULSIVE COMPARISON**</u>

I was told he wasn't attracted to me physically,
he just wants to stay friends with me for the intelligent
conversation.
His past girlfriends were all disloyal or
nymphomaniacs without discretion,
so…I just don't get it.
He said "You must have some understanding of this,
look at the two men you gave a rejection notice."
No…**I cannot agree,**
those examples were totally inadequate.
One does not brush his teeth which are blackened and
rotten,
unclinical hygiene is an abomination!!!
The other wanted a replacement mother,
and it's **not my job** to shelter and raise him.
After all, by law he is an adult,
but I see a boy in the place of a man.

PLEASE!!!

These are unfair and repulsive comparisons.
I have some semblance of class,
knowing inside and out that I am a vision of beauty
and you are truly a blind man.
I would have treated you like a king and so much
more,
because in my eyes you could do no wrong as someone
I adored.
But you said no LOUD AND CLEAR,
your insults still echo in my ears.

POISONOUS ROSE PETALS

She was the envy of every female there except me,
when she became the recipient of a dozen roses and
chocolate candy.
Well – she is my friend, I adore her like a sister.
But I know where those roses originated from;
she'll be PAYING FOR IT later.
I shook my head in disbelief,
(more so in sorrow)
at the joy dancing in her eyes now,
replaced with misery and grief tomorrow.
You see, her admirer is wicked;
nothing she ever does is unselfish.
She expects every "act of goodwill" to go repaid in
full,
and when it is not she is "very disappointed".
If you think you don't owe her any favors for doing
something nice,
do yourself a favor and don't turn your back, you just
might find her **knife** in it.

Spike Bloodworth

NOWHERE TO SLEEP AT SUNSET

Let me tell you a tale of poverty and relay the day's
events,
of two homeless people with nowhere to sleep at
sunset.
The people around them are much colder than the
winter streets,
and should their roles be reversed they would beg to
return to a richer way of living.
Today we wake at 5 A.M. to dine on water and bread,
pacing the walks to keep warm and beg.
Thick clothes are a blessing in the winter yet also a
burden in the summer,
once a week comes our priveledge to shower.
Tonight we dine on water and bread,
sleep in a subway or on a hardwood floor for a bed.
We wake again at 5 A.M.,
to dine on water and bread and search for a new place
to sleep at sunset.

<u>DAGGERS</u>

What on Earth is wrong with me?
Why don't I think before I speak?
Everything she did wrong was driving me crazy,
all I wanted was peace and tranquility.
I didn't want to destroy her and make her feel
unwelcome,
but I told her I hate her and that's just the kind of
damage I had done.
I hurt her feelings,
made her cry.
Innocent as she was she believed me,
I did'nt really mean it at the time.
I guess I have forgotten how to think like a child,
how love is all that really matters.
How words can wound the very soul,
ripping it to pieces like daggers.

<u>VENOM</u>

Alone in his hospital bed,
drowning in his own self pity;
saturated in despair,
he finally decides he needs me.
I was there for him despite his neglect before he landed
in that bed,
but he was always somewhere else when I desperately
needed a friend.
I won't apologize for my icy bedside manner,
since I could not care less even if I was paid to care.
I can't pamper a wounded man without love for me to
share.
Maybe it's time that he knew that the time has finally
come;
for him to suffer the very same that I suffer from:
veins full of venom.

<u>SAVAGES</u>

If death were equal to death criminals would think
again,
that is not penalty but disciplinary action.
Who am I to step in and judge?
perhaps the next victim of a savage.
I care nothing of revenge but aspire for the power of
prevention,
since only in a lawless society does a rapist or
murderer walk free.
They slay the innocent for savage amusement,
bathing in the blood of the slain.
In essence we are all just walking targets,
waiting in line for the deliverance of pain.

Spike Bloodworth

<u>LEPROSY</u>

There's completely no intimacy,
absolutely no sign of love.
Friendships are far and few,
never am I touched.
Always I ask myself what makes me so undesirable,
what abomination have I done?
I desperately await an answer,
that answer never comes.
The more I reach out the more they move away,
as if getting too close wears out my welcome to stay.
All I need is human kindness,
kindness so few appreciate.
Prized like gold is affection and a genuine smile,
deeply am I yearning for some company who isn't
afraid to stay awhile.
Wilted is the generosity that goes unshared,
seldom does it surface when the recipient is prepared.
Just a little pinch of sentiment would be enough,
from someone – ANYONE!!!
Forever tarnished is my understanding of love,
since I've never been that close to anyone.
There's a beautiful butterfly trapped inside of me,
waiting for positive reinforcement to release and set it
free.
Only a heart so alone and empty could suffer the
symptoms of leprosy.

PLAIN JANE

She's nothing special to look at,
nothing exceptional to write home about.
Just a regular Plain Jane,
you know I even forgot her name.
He chose her over me,
it made me fume and growl,
nevertheless it was better to leave the matter alone
entirely.
It burned me to a feverish pitch to see the two together,
to abstain from giving any hint of recognition.
I entertained the thought of dumping a pitcher of cold
water over his head,
and refraining from doing so left me with a feeling of
dissatisfaction.
Once again <u>mine</u> was Cupid's pen.
As their presence ruined my evening,
I wish the night I had loaned it to them that pen ran out
of ink!

Spike Bloodworth

PURGE – ATORY

She said her tummy hurt but I didn't believe her,
she's always been the stubborn type who refuses to eat
her dinner.
So mistakenly thinking this evening was no different,
I continuously proceeded to feed her.
I should've listened to this child when she announced
"I do not feel well."
but then again there is no surefire way to tell.
Well as you may have predicted here is the moral of
the story:
she ran to the bathroom heaving toward purge-atory.

<u>SCANDALOUS!</u>

Strangers invade your privacy with intent toward
malice,
the pitfalls of humiliation make your life so
scandalous!
When you're caught up in their snares life becomes
stranger than fiction,
and they drudge up damaging details about you merely
for entertainment purposes.
Whatever seemed the right thing to do at the time,
now is just a living, breathing nightmare.
It's breathing down your neck day and night,
and you seriously wonder how it got there.

Spike Bloodworth

<u>SPLINTERS</u>

They're so beautiful together,
inseparable and perfectly united lovers.
I can see the synchronicity of feeling,
the closeness of their unity.
I wish a man looked at me the way he looks at her,
as if there's nothing he's adored more.
He probably isn't even aware of it,
that he can't keep his eyes off of her.
But she does the same so who really cares?
I doubt either of them notice the others in the
backdrop,
not much else matters.
It's touching to witness,
but sometimes it still hurts.
Her safety is his deepest concern,
it keeps her smile glowing warm.
My heart is envious,
convulsing in splinters.
I have to turn my head away,
before the tears flow and burn.
Hm. some friend I am!
And I can only hope the pain stays well hidden.
It's not that I don't wish the best for them both,
with neither was I ever involved.
It's just when I was convinced there's no such thing as
love,
well around the next bend they come.
What a struggle to watch!
to pick out the splinters one by one.

<u>VIVACEOUS</u>

Where are you now that I've got a life?
Where are you hiding instead of running wild
with me side by side?
How can you hesitate to live a life this fine?
Where is the excitement in your eyes?
I can't leave you breathless in the dust.
You need a sudden pick - me - up.
and when all is said and done,
all you will remember is having fun!
So come on! hurry up!
Don't make me beg and grab your arm,
coaxing and pleading and dragging you along.
second chances don't happen enough.

Spike Bloodworth

<u>NO PRESSURE</u>

"Don't feel any pressure – really – just take your time
on it."
"Just making you aware it needs to get done – at
increments - at your leisure."
Ever take a close look at the orator's posture?
they shrink lower and lower with each statement;
while it makes them uncomfortable to be the bearer of
bad news,
behind the **abrubt** changes.
They are trying to be nonthreatening and polite,
to motivate you to really **pick up the pace.**
Attempting to make it look like a free will choice,
thus whether you like it or not it needs to be done in
great haste.
I still respect this approach,
they are requesting that a need be filled.
Perhaps the orator feels the lack of authority to be in
the position to present ultimatums,
and this particular approach is not used often enough.

<u>IT COMES TO YOU DIRECT</u>

Sometimes you look at me like I grabbed you hard on
the arm,
because I brought your world to a screeching halt.
What I have to convey to you I must communicate to
you this very second,
it is too important to wait another minute.
It is my responsibility for now to pass this message
along,
what you do with it from here is your business.
But I will be resilient and will not relent until I have had
my say,
it really is that detrimental to your existence.
I may very well save you some trouble in the end if
you simply stop and listen,
because otherwise don't you think there are other
things I could also being doing?
Don't you think there is a long list of things I should be
accomplishing of equal importance?
of course there is!
Be glad I bothered to do this now before it was too
late,
then you would've blamed me because your luck
would not have been the same.
Instead I made you a priority,
now act on the information I gave you accordingly.

Spike Bloodworth

<u>BURIED ALIVE</u>

He stared at me with that lordly look on his face
(so numb and impersonal),
then shrugged off all my sentiments and made me feel
uncomfortable.
The muscles in my throat tighten with urgency to
scream,
to grab him by the lapels and shout at him
"Say something – anything!"
But he is the epitomy of control with the reserve of
steel,
and once that has taken hold he shows nothing of what
he feels.
And now there is no chemistry between us like there
once was,
only his confining boundaries that nail the lid to my
box.
Sometimes he'll shrug off the slightest touch,
or if I move too close he will instantly get up.
More importantly his silence smothers me,
this sudden distorted blockade between he and I –
that in itself is what keeps me buried alive.

PRY YOU AWAY

Every time I try to speak with you
she pries away your attention;
runs right over to where we stand,
and competes for all your central focus.
She has done it so often for so many years,
I'm sure it's entirely innocent;
maybe even unintentional or unconscientious.
Whatever her reasons it does a number on our
friendship,
because she comes off overbearing and protective.
If she includes you everywhere she goes and you
include her,
you might as well be Siamese twins.
I cannot will myself to allow myself to be compared to
her and be overshadowed,
to come short of her apparent perfection.
That's a hard act to follow,
because you clearly kiss the ground she walks on.
No one surrounding you would dare interfere,
because you clearly adore this woman.
You are a great guy to know,
but I assume she knows you much better.
My welcome has worn off by now,
so the farther away I stay will keep her content forever.

Spike Bloodworth

<u>BONDAGE</u>

I'm everywhere you go,
everywhere you'll be,
in every direction,
I am all that you will see.
My goal is suffocation,
you have no room to breathe.
I am attached to you like a siamese twin,
together at last and never separated.
Don't try to lose me I will always find you,
like a bloodhound following in hot pursuit.
My name strikes fear in the heart of the hunted,
the hunted…meaning you.
This is your life in bondage,
you don't want forever but **<u>I</u>** DO.

TAPPING THE VEINS

Three hours on the examination table,
to check for contamination.
They have to be so careful now,
that's the process of elimination.
You offer your precious limbs to carve up like a
turkey,
puncture your pressure points while you're dying for
the money.
Just think about the life you give to another human
being,
a glorious sentiment – but only secondary.
The needle burns going in, burns going out,
you'll grin and bear it somehow.
On a bi-weekly basis you are tapping the veins,
juicing the pulp out of what little remains.
God only knows your suffering, desperation and pain;
nevertheless, soon you'll be there running on empty
again.

BITTER AFTER-TASTE

I held you in the highest regards and loved you like a
mother,
saintly woman who offered us shelter.
You were the ultimate authority on patient endeavors,
while showing us the beauty of nature and warmth of
your home.
Angel of light for the meekest and weak,
you showed us the way to knowledge and wisdom.
If given the chance I would bow down at your feet,
but I cannot give you back your grand daughter.
You are not alone – I also loved her.
This choice I made was not choice at all.
Both of us suffer.
If she had stayed with me my child had no future,
I could not withhold a plentiful home from her much
longer.
I cannot blame you for feeling bitter,
I did not only lose my daughter I lost so much more:
I lost all my loved ones and my greatest teacher.

<u>IGOR</u>

Igor fetch this and Igor fetch that,
she is somehow inferior but ever so glad.
Igor wants to be your sidekick,
the best you ever had.
Igor is a good servant if she caters to her man,
so please your master if you really think you can.
I hear the bells ringing,
hear your fingers snap,
Igor didn't come when he called,
BAD! BAD! BAD!
I bet you think I will stand right here and let you slap
my hand,
but you can't bite the hand that feeds or it will bite you
back!
You say Igor is pitiful, useless and ugly.
Maybe I am smarter than you think and you are just
damn lucky.
So let's get this straight Victor Frankenstein Jr.
Igor finds you disgusting and downright insulting.

Spike Bloodworth

<u>THE STRANGLER</u>

Sisters living in fear under parental tyranny wanting to
run away or somehow be free.
They wander through the childhood years in misguided
anxiety,
starving for love and terribly lonely.
They reach out to unsupportive figures of authority,
wishing their dreams could rescue them from the
restrictive lives they lead.
The angst builds without release…
Sisters pitted against each other for parental
amusement,
in a competition so bitter their bond was annihilated.
One fatal day one sister exploded at the other,
her iron tight grasp applying death grip pressure.
The offender was gasping for breath in total surrender,
living to see another day to breathe the open air.
The offender never forgave her seething sibling.
(I cannot reconcile the offender from her woes.)
I do not blame her in the least if forgiveness never
comes,
Although I have offered sincere apologies stemming
from remorse.

<u>MOMMY WHERE IS DADDY?</u>

"Mommy where is daddy? does he love me?"
"No child, he doesn't love you or any other human
being."
I watch you suffer as you reach out for your father,
only to come back rejected and empty handed.
You reprimand me for your existence,
forlorn and broken hearted.
"Mommy where is daddy? why won't he come to see
me?"
"Honey, he despises us both because you are living
and breathing."
"Little one – he is unreliable but you will always have
mommy."

THE BETRAYAL

She never suspected I wasn't there with her,
and if she awakened it would've distressed the girl.
I left her alone,
risking obvious dangers.
I alone knew she was unattended,
but I was overwhelmed with the dire need to be selfish.
That is the point of the betrayal,
here it all is.
When I returned she was still embraced in slumber,
just the way I had left her.
A police car cruised by on our street,
I was so fortunate my little angel wasn't in it.
In repentance the morning after I swore to myself,
NEVER AGAIN,
NEVER AGAIN.

DON'T MAKE ME REPEAT MYSELF

My angry mother leans over to me and asks "What did
you just say?" and as I open my mouth to answer she
slaps me in the face.
"That answer isn't good enough and now I want the
truth, and if you lie to me you'll get it worse."
So I said what I had to say regardless how much it
hurt.
It is no small wonder we discerned for ourselves the
difference between right and wrong.
But we did and we knew it all along.
What mother wanted to hear was her own words
coming from my mouth,
something definitely opposite the truth, that never
came out.
I never gave her the satisfaction of making me cry.
It made me sick to see her with that vengeful look in
her eyes.
The moral of the story is:
All is well that ends well.
So do your best to hear me the first time and don't
make me repeat myself!

ABOUT THE AUTHOR

Spike Bloodworth was originally born under the name
Desiree Daniella Bloodworth.
She was raised in California.
After high school graduation she traveled nonstop
throughout the U.S.
A homeless transient most of her lifetime.
In the year 1992 her daughter Monica was born,
later to be given up for adoption at the age of 6.
Currently Spike resides in Denver Colorado in hopeful
pursuit of helpful ways to assist the hearing impaired.